Meet the
ARIZONA
CARDINALS

BY
ZACK BURGESS

NORWOODHOUSE 🏠 PRESS

CHICAGO, ILLINOIS

NORWOODHOUSE PRESS

P.O. Box 316598 • Chicago, Illinois 60631
For more information about Norwood House Press please visit our website at
www.norwoodhousepress.com or call 866-565-2900.

Photo Credits:
All photos courtesy of Associated Press, except for the following: Topps, Inc. (6, 10 bottom, 11 top & middle), Bowman Gum Co. (10 top), The Upper Deck Co. (11 bottom), Black Book Archives (18, 23), Ziff-Davis (22).

Cover Photo: Tom Hauck/Associated Press

The football memorabilia photographed for this book is part of the authors' collection. The collectibles used for artistic background purposes in this series were manufactured by many different card companies— including Bowman, Donruss, Fleer, Leaf, O-Pee-Chee, Pacific, Panini America, Philadelphia Chewing Gum, Pinnacle, Pro Line, Pro Set, Score, Topps, and Upper Deck—as well as several food brands, including Crane's, Hostess, Kellogg's, McDonald's and Post.

Designer: Ron Jaffe
Series Editors: Mike Kennedy and Mark Stewart
Project Management: Black Book Partners, LLC.
Editorial Production: Lisa Walsh

LIBRARY OF CONGRESS CATALOGING-IN-PUBLICATION DATA
Names: Burgess, Zack.
Title: Meet the Arizona Cardinals / by Zack Burgess.
Description: Chicago, Illinois : Norwood House Press, [2016] | Series: Big picture sports | Includes bibliographical references and index. | Audience: Grade: K to Grade 3.
Identifiers: LCCN 2015024581| ISBN 9781599537283 (library ed.) | ISBN 9781603578318 (ebook)
Subjects: LCSH: Arizona Cardinals (Football team)--Miscellanea--Juvenile literature.
Classification: LCC GV956.A75 B87 2016 | DDC 796.332/640979173--dc23 LC record available at http://lccn.loc.gov/2015024581

288N—072016
Manufactured in the United States of America in North Mankato, Minnesota

CONTENTS

Words in **bold type** are defined on page 24.

The Cardinals have lots of fun on the field.

CALL ME A CARDINAL

Cardinals are beautiful red birds. They are known for keeping a sharp eye on their territory. The same is true about the Arizona Cardinals. They are tough on defense, and also fun to watch on offense. The "Cards" can take off at a moment's notice.

Karlos
Dansby

TIME MACHINE

The Cardinals are one of the oldest teams in the National Football League (NFL). Their first home was Chicago, Illinois. They moved to Missouri, and later to Arizona. Now the Cardinals play in the city of Phoenix. The team has always relied on great quarterbacks, including **Jim Hart** and Kurt Warner.

Jim
HART
ST. LOUIS CARDS • Q'BACK

Kurt Warner spots an open receiver.

The Cardinals love playing on real grass.

Best Seat in the House

Frank

The Cardinals play in an indoor stadium with a real grass field. How does the grass grow? The field can be rolled outside to get the sunlight it needs. Cardinals fans believe their stadium is the best in the NFL.

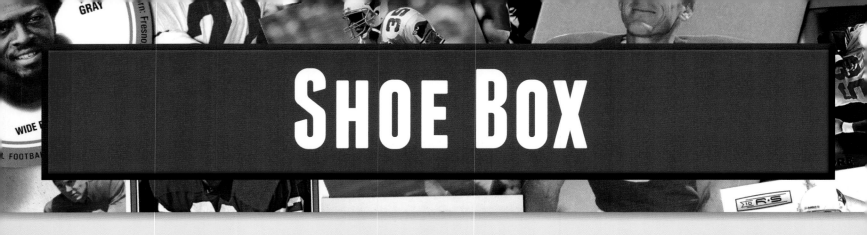

The trading cards on these pages show some of the best Cardinals ever.

CHARLEY TRIPPI

RUNNING BACK & QUARTERBACK · 1947-1955

Charley was the Cardinals' top star when they played in Chicago. He was the hero of the 1947 NFL Championship Game.

LARRY WILSON

SAFETY · 1960-1972

Larry was the leader of the team's defense. He was an **All-Pro** five times.

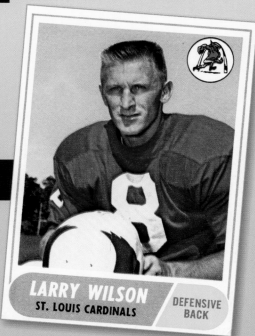

LARRY WILSON
ST. LOUIS CARDINALS
DEFENSIVE BACK

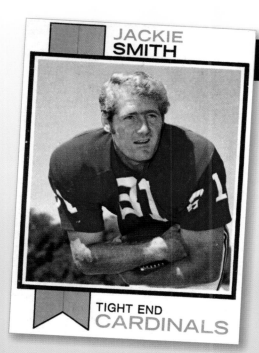

JACKIE SMITH

TIGHT END · 1963-1977

Jackie was a great blocker and pass receiver. He used his big body to create space for himself on the field.

ROY GREEN

RECEIVER · 1979-1990

Roy started as a defensive back. When the Cardinals moved him to receiver, he became a superstar.

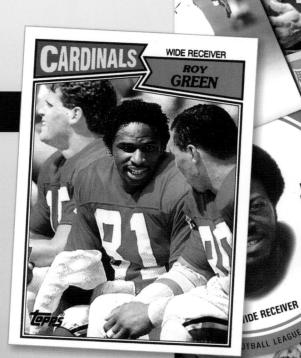

AENEAS WILLIAMS

CORNERBACK · 1991-2000

Aeneas stuck to receivers like glue. He returned six **interceptions** for touchdowns for the Cardinals.

11

THE BIG PICTURE

Look at the two photos on page 13. Both appear to be the same. But they are not. There are three differences. Can you spot them?

Answers on page 23.

13

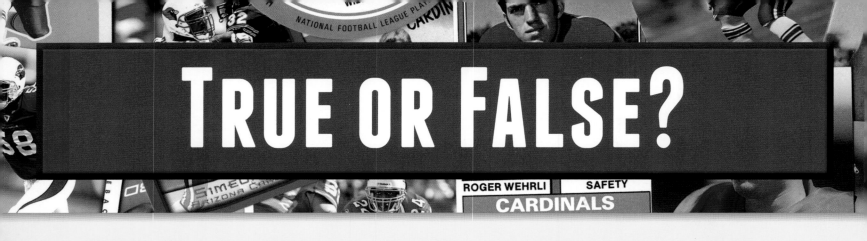

TRUE OR FALSE?

Larry Fitzgerald was a star receiver. Two of these facts about him are **TRUE**. One is **FALSE**. Do you know which is which?

1 Larry made the **Pro Bowl** every year from 2007 to 2013.

2 Larry's mother was a champion cliff diver.

3 Larry set a record with 30 catches in the 2008 **postseason**.

Answer on page 23.

Larry Fitzgerald scans the defense after catching a pass.

15

The Cardinals get amazing support from their fans.

Go Cardinals, Go!

Cardinals fans love to wear red. On game day, the stadium is known as the "Red Sea." The crowd can get very noisy. The excitement starts when the team sounds the Big Red Siren before kickoff. The fans keep cheering until the clock runs out.

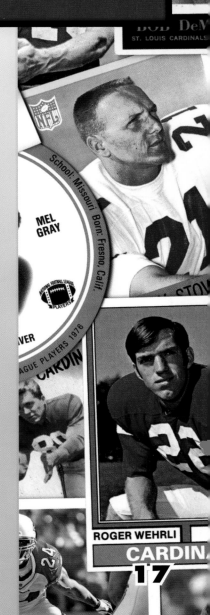

ON THE MAP

Here is a look at where five Cardinals were born, along with a fun fact about each.

 1 PAT TILLMAN · FREMONT, CALIFORNIA
A statue of Pat stands outside the Cardinals' stadium. It honors his heroics in the army.

 2 LARRY CENTERS · TATUM, TEXAS ●━━━━━━▶
Larry made the Pro Bowl in 1995 and 1996.

 3 JIM HART · EVANSTON, ILLINOIS
Jim threw 209 touchdown passes for the Cardinals.

 4 ANQUAN BOLDIN · PAHOKEE, FLORIDA
Anquan had 217 receiving yards in his first NFL game.

 5 MIKE DAWSON · DORKING, ENGLAND
Mike played defensive end for the Cardinals in St. Louis for seven seasons.

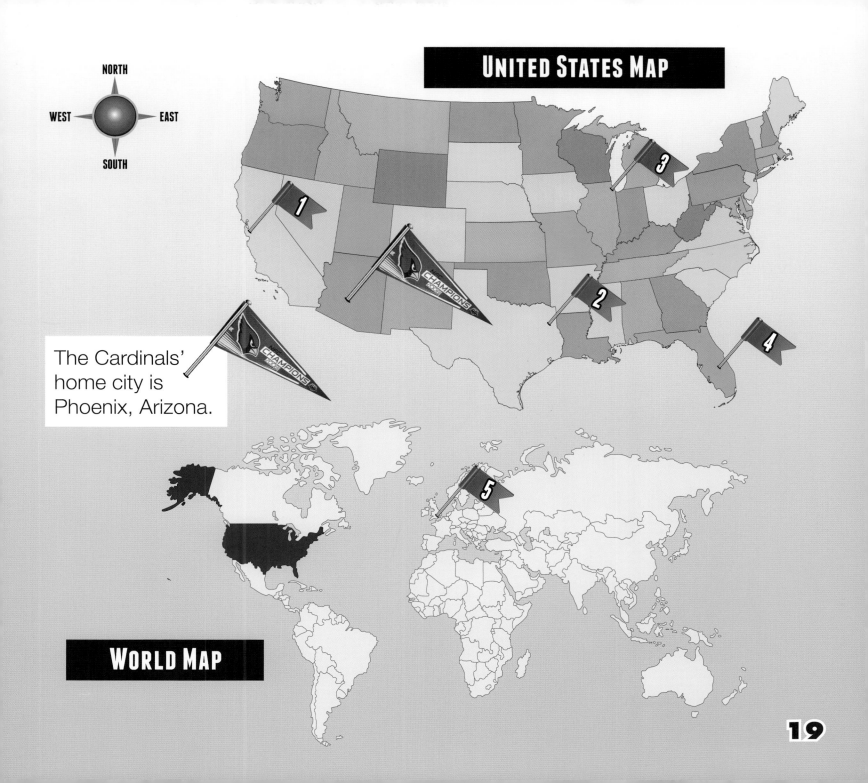

NORTH

WEST — EAST

SOUTH

1

3

2

4

The Cardinals' home city is Phoenix, Arizona.

CHAMPIONS

CHAMPIONS

5

WORLD MAP

19

HOME AND AWAY

David Johnson wears the Cardinals' home uniform.

Football teams wear different uniforms for home and away games. The main colors of the Cardinals are red and white. The team's red jerseys are among the most colorful in the NFL.

Patrick Peterson wears the Cardinals' away uniform.

The team's helmet hasn't changed much since the 1960s. It shows a cardinal's head on each side. The Cardinals are one of just a few NFL teams to use a white helmet.

21

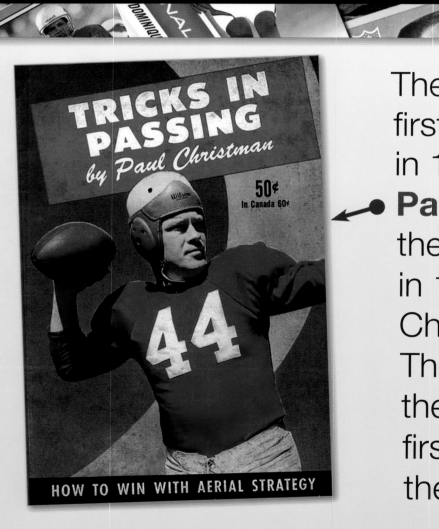

The Cardinals won their first NFL championship in 1925. Quarterback **Paul Christman** led them to their second, in 1947. They played in Chicago both seasons. The Cardinals reached the Super Bowl for the first time at the end of the 2008 season.

RECORD BOOK

These Cardinals set team records.

TOUCHDOWN PASSES		RECORD
Season:	Carson Palmer (2015)	35
Career:	Jim Hart	209

TOUCHDOWN CATCHES		RECORD
Season:	**Sonny Randle** (1960)	15
Career:	Larry Fitzgerald	98

RUSHING TOUCHDOWNS		RECORD
Season:	John David Crow (1962)	14
Career:	Ottis Anderson	46

ANSWERS FOR THE BIG PICTURE
The logo was removed from #38's helmet, #5 was turned upside-down, and the football changed to a basketball.

ANSWER FOR TRUE AND FALSE
#2 is false. Larry's mother was not a champion cliff diver.

FOOTBALL WORDS

INDEX

All-Pro
An honor given to the best NFL player at each position.

Interceptions
Passes caught by a defensive player.

Postseason
The games played after the regular season, including the Super Bowl.

Pro Bowl
The NFL's annual all-star game.

Photos are on **BOLD** numbered pages.

ABOUT THE AUTHOR

Zack Burgess has been writing about sports for more than 20 years. He has lived all over the country and interviewed lots of All-Pro football players, including Brett Favre, Eddie George, Jerome Bettis, Shannon Sharpe, and Rich Gannon. Zack was the first African American beat writer to cover Major League Baseball when he worked for the *Kansas City Star*.

ABOUT THE CARDINALS

Learn more at these websites:

www.azcardinals.com • www.profootballhof.com

www.teamspiritextras.com/Overtime/html/cardinals.html